6.99

A CHILD'S BOOK OF PRAYERS

Chariot Books is an imprint of David C. Cook Publishing Co.
David C. Cook Publishing Co., Elgin, Illinois 60120
David C. Cook Publishing Co., Weston, Ontario

A CHILD'S BOOK OF PRAYERS

Designed by Wayne Hanna

First printing, 1987
Printed in Singapore
91 90   5 4 3

All Scripture quotations in this publication are from the Holy
Bible, New International Version. Copyright © 1973, 1978, 1984,
International Bible Society. Used by permission of Zondervan
Bible Publishers.

Library of Congress Cataloging-in-Publication Data

Tangvald, Christine Harder, 1941
   A child's book of prayers.

   Summary: A collection of simple prayers accompanied by
Scripture verses and illustrations.
   1. Children—Prayer books and devotions—English. [1. Prayer
books and devotions] I. Hook, Frances, ill. II. Hook, Richard, ill.
III. Title.
BV265.T4   1987   242'.82   86-32971
ISBN 1-55513-677-X

A CHILD'S BOOK OF PRAYERS

Illustrated by
FRANCES and RICHARD HOOK

WRITTEN BY
CHRISTINE HARDER TANGVALD

Chariot Books
DAVID C. COOK PUBLISHING CO.

Where are you, God?
I can't see you,
but I know you are there.

You are always there when I need you
. . . and I need you all of the time!

Now faith is being sure of what we hope for
and certain of what we do not see.

Hebrews 11:1

*J*esus,
I feel SAFE
because I know you love me.
I'm glad you love me.
I love you, too.

The Lord will keep you from all harm—
he will watch over your life.

Psalm 121:7

*T*his tiny flower is so beautiful.

God, you not only made the
BIG important things,
you made the LITTLE important things,
too.

I like little things, God.
Thank you for this tiny flower.

In the beginning God created the heavens
and the earth. God saw all that he had made,
and it was very good.

Genesis 1:1, 31

*Y*ou have the WHOLE WORLD
in your hands, Lord.
Here is *my* hand.
We will walk with you and
talk with you, and
we will all be friends.

Dear friends, since God so loved us,
we also ought to love one another.

I John 4:11

$\mathcal{J}$esus, when I am SORRY,
you forgive me, don't you?
You understand how I feel.

I hope my mom and dad understand . . .
when I am sorry.

If we confess our sins, he is faithful and just
and will forgive us our sins
and purify us from all unrighteousness.

I John 1:9

*J*esus, I tell my friends about you.
I tell them that you live
in heaven with God.

If we believe in you,
we can live in heaven someday, too
. . . with YOU!

Jesus said . . . "I am the resurrection
and the life. He who believes in me will live,
even though he dies."

John 11:25

*H*ere are my hands to work for you.
Help them be good in all they do.
Thank you for food to make me strong
To work for you all day long.

You will have plenty to eat,
until you are full,
and you will praise the name
of the Lord your God.

Joel 2:26

*J*esus, I learned from the Bible
that you walked on *top* of the water!
How could you *do* that?
It was a miracle, right?
You could do it because you are GOD.

I like learning about your miracles,
Jesus.

Jesus did many other things as well.
If every one of them were written down,
I suppose that even the whole world would not
have room for the books that would be written.

John 21:25

1 like you, and
you like me!
Isn't that right, Jesus?

You even said so.
You said, "Let the little children
    come to me."
I'm glad you like little children
    . . . LIKE ME!

Jesus said, "Let the little children
come to me, and do not hinder them,
for the kingdom of heaven belongs
to such as these."

Matthew 19:14

God, you colored our world
bright and beautiful.
You splashed our days with sunshine.
You made butterflies and rainbows.

I like your blues and greens
and reds and yellows.
Can you guess which color is
my favorite?

Thank you, God, for pretty colors.

This is the day the Lord has made;
let us rejoice and be glad in it.

Psalm 118:24

1 need your love, Lord.

Forgive me when I'm bad.
Help me when I'm lonely or sad.

Every day, in every way,
I need your love.

The Lord is gracious and compassionate,
slow to anger and rich in love.

Psalm 145:8

*S*isters and brothers!
We are good friends.

We play together.
We think together.
Sometimes we pray together.

Thank you, God, for
sisters and brothers.

A friend loves at all times.

Proverbs 17:17

*T*hank you for my mother, Jesus.
You had a nice mother, too,
didn't you?
Aren't mothers WONDERFUL?
Thank you for *my* mother, Jesus.

"Honor your father and mother . . .
that it may go well with you and that
you may enjoy long life on the earth."

Ephesians 6:2, 3

*A*ll day and
all night.
Watch over me, Lord.
Keep me safe and
stay with me.
All day and
all night.

The Lord watches over you . . .
the sun will not harm you by day,
nor the moon by night.

Psalm 121:5, 6